LUCA MOZZATI

POMPEII

VIRTUAL RECONSTRUCTION
OF SITES AND MONUMENTS

MONDADORI

© 2013 Mondadori Electa S.p.A., Milano
Mondadori Libri Illustrati
All rights reserved
www.librimondadori.it

INDEX

HISTORIC EVENTS AND THE DEVELOPMENT OF THE CITY

1. The eruption

"A cloud formed, whose aspect and shape can best be described as resembling a pine tree...huge flames and great tongues of fire rose from many points on Mount Vesuvius...". This is how Pliny the Younger, writing from Cape Misenum, described the terrifying eruption of Vesuvius to the historian Tacitus: an eruption which lasted from August 24th to 26th in 79 A.D. Thanks to Pliny, we also know that the seismic tremors preceding the disaster did not alarm the inhabitants of Herculaneum, Stabiae and Pompeii, who were so used to such movements of the Earth that they did not even interrupt their daily routine. The destruction was horrendous, and the operations organized by Emperor Titus to remedy the damage had little effect. Probably some precious objects were salvaged, but then the area descended into silence and the town of Pompeii lost even its name. It was left to the archaeologists to rediscover this old city in the Campania. Paradoxically, this catastrophe, by covering everything in mud and ashes, has provided us with the chance to experience the life of a Roman city with amazing fidelity. Excavations began in 1748, and excited passionate enthusiasm throughout Europe, influencing artistic output and making an important contribution to the birth of Neoclassicism.

TIMELINE

abt 1500 B.C. settlements in Pompeian area documented by necropolises	**753 B.C.** foundation of Rome		**VII-VI century** expansion in the Campania of Southern Etruscans settled in Capua and of Greek colonists from Ischia	**474 B.C.** the Greco-Syracusan fleet defeats the Etruscan one in the war for the control over the Campania		**343-290 B.C.** Samnite Wars
1500 B.C.	800 B.C.	700 B.C.	600 B.C.	500 B.C.	400 B.C.	300 B.C.
	abt 770 B.C. foundation of the Greek colony of Pithekoussai on the island of Ischia	**VI century B.C.** building of a shrine dedicated to Apollo, of the Doric Temple and of a circle of wall in Pompeii. Possible control of the Auruncians over Pompeii, open to cultural exchanges.			**V century B.C.** Samnite control over Pompeii	

2. The multi-ethnic city

Pompeii was built on a plateau created by an old lava flow, standing at about 30 metres above sea level and in a dominating position above the Sarno valley: an excellent location for a town dependent on port access. There is evidence of settlements in the area going back to 1500 B.C., and some information about these has been gleaned from the necropolises. From the 8th century B.C. onwards, with the establishment of the Greek colony of Pithekoussai on the island of Ischia, the region became involved in trading between the Greeks, the Phoenicians, the Etruscans (settled in Capua) and the Samnites in the hinterland. From the 6th century, various places of worship were built in prominent positions, including a shrine to Apollo and another possibly to Heracles. These were surrounded by a wall built of tuff, to protect commercial trading activity. Evidence of a stable presence of both Greeks and Etruscans in Pompeii has led to a lively debate over who actually held political control of the city.

One can deduce that the geographical position of the town would have encouraged the settlement there of both these peoples alongside the native Auruncians, who benefited from their building techniques and absorbed their cults, blending them with the local ones. Of this archaic phase of construction, with structures in perishable materials such as wood and mud bricks, no trace remains.

		89 B.C. Sulla besieges Pompeii, which capitulates after a strenuous resistance	**59 A.D.** brawl in the amphitheatre between the Pompeians and the Nucerians	**79 A.D.** 24th August: Vesuvius begins to erupt		**1748** first archaeological excavations
264-146 B.C. Punic Wars						

200 B.C.	**100 B.C.**	**0**	**100 A.D.**	**1700 A.D.**	

	91-88 B.C. Social War	**80 B.C.** Sulla gathers in Pompeii a colony of his veterans. Pax Romana is established	**62 A.D.** a devastating earthquake severely damages Pompeii. Reconstruction work is still in progress at the time of the eruption

3. The Samnite period

After the victory of the Greco-Syracusan fleet over that of the Etruscans in 474 B.C., the walls of Pompeii were reinforced with a double circle of limestone blocks, supported by four-sided towers. Between the 5th and 4th centuries B.C., the old centre of the town (characterized by its irregular layout and extending around the area of the forum and of the "Triangular Forum") was expanded using a Hellenic orthogonal design. However this cannot be taken as a definite sign of Greek hegemony. It is more credible that the Samnites, who were extending their control over the Campania plain, had also imposed their supremacy on Pompeii, as indicated by various inscriptions in the Oscan language. It was also probably these Italic people who began to develop the city vertically, with interlinked buildings, and to reinforce the walls with an agger (rampart) and new towers.

Samnite control endured a long conflict with Rome, which, following the victory over Hannibal, had managed to achieve supremacy over the whole Mediterranean basin. This expansion of the boundaries of the Romanized world brought with it a

Via di Mercurio. Buildings with decorations in first style

growth in the commercial life of Pompeii, and the town was affected by cultural influences reflected in improvements in building techniques. More stone buildings were built, including houses of large size, to replace the austere Samnite dwellings. They were embellished with architectural elements and decorative features in the Hellenistic tradition, as in the sumptuous "House of the Faun".

4. The Roman colony

Pompeii remained loyal to Rome during the Social War. After this ended, however, Sulla besieged and occupied the town, and in 80 B.C. transformed it into a Roman colony under the name of Cornelia Veneria Pompeianorum, imposing it about 2,000 veterans. The Dictator constructed a magnificent marble temple, dedicated to Venus, near Marina Gate, so extending it outwards towards the sea. In the years that followed, many houses inside and outside the town were radically modernized in the Roman style, although the population of Samnite origin remained loyal to the more austere, Italic style of building. A number of indications, including the way in which the old judiciary continued to survive alongside the new, demonstrate how the process of Romanization

Arch of Caligula and Via di Mercurio

developed gradually and without any sudden trauma. This period saw the construction of a new covered theatre, of modest size; a new bath complex near the Forum, to complement the Stabian Baths established by the Samnites; and a further facility, more modern in design, outside Marina Gate. However, the most important operations involved the reconstruction of the Temple of Jupiter Capitoline in the Forum to a Roman design, and the building of an amphitheatre (the oldest stone-built example currently known), designed to satisfy the Samnite appetite for gladiatorial games. The number of luxury homes increased, while the method of decoration developed along the so-called "four styles" of wall painting. This situation indicates a general state of wellbeing in the population and an absence of marked social differences, attributable to the absence of any large estates and to the presence, of medium-sized farming and artisan businesses.

The process of Romanization is demonstrated in a series of architectural projects which confirm the imperial cult: the rebuilding of the Temples of Jupiter and Apollo; the construction of the Sanctuary of the Lares, the Temple of Vespasian, the Temple of Fortuna Augusta, and the Building of Eumachia. There were also altars dedicated to the emperors inside private homes, and statues erected in the Forum and other public places.

Finally, the construction of the aqueduct transformed the quality of life for the citizens of Pompeii, replacing the ancient wells and taking water to the baths and many public water fountains, as well as to the more luxurious homes, which had their own baths and water outlets.

The many earthquakes, and particularly the one in 62 A.D., caused considerable damage to public and private buildings. At the time of the eruption in 79 A.D., there were building sites everywhere. In many of the more prestigious dwellings, the restoration work involved transforming part of the

Vicolo Storto, with a fountain and a water tower

structure into workshops or shops to rent, in an attempt to recuperate part of the cost of the operations. The situation revealed by the excavations, therefore, is that of a city tragically assaulted at the very time when its more than twenty thousand inhabitants were in the process of rebuilding it, displaying their perseverance and tenacity.

The east side of the Forum, along Via di Mercurio
facing the Sanctuary of Lares. On the right, the Macellum,
in the middle the Temple of Jupiter Capitoline

THE HOME OF THE REPUBLICAN AGE

The oldest houses in Pompeii date back to the 4th and 3rd centuries B.C., or the middle of the Samnite era. These are buildings which conform to the Italic style of construction, centring on an atrium. A corridor divided into two parts gave access to the house. The first part, the *vestibulum*, was interrupted from the entrance gate, then the corridor took the name of *fauces* and led to a large central space (*atrium*) on which opened environments of different sizes. A system of movable screens was provided to prevent indiscreet glimpses, and a strong grating to discourage burglars. There was often a kitchen garden behind the house, for growing vegetables, fruit, and also vines and olive trees, to provide wine and oil. The outer surface of the house was bare, with few openings: light came through the partially exposed atrium. This had a four-sided roof sloping towards the central area (*compluvium*), which channelled rain water into an underground cistern (*impluvium*), ensuring a ready supply for the house. This type of atrium with the sections

of the roof converging inwards is known as the "Tuscan" type, and is common in Pompeii. Other variants include: the testudinate atrium, without a central opening, the tetrastyle atrium, with the roof resting on four columns, and the Corinthian atrium, featuring more columns.

The bedrooms (*cubicula*) and vestibules (*alae*) were arranged around the central hall. Opposite the entrance, there was a large room (*tablinum*), which served as a sitting room and reception area. This led into the garden at the back, and could be screened off by curtains or movable partitions.

The name *atrium* is derived from *ater*, meaning black or dark, and this tells us that it was originally the site of the hearth and focal point of the house.

The atrium also housed the *lararium*, the altar dedicated to the lares, the protective deities of the house. Over time, the atrium also became the place for receiving guests, in particular supporters of rich householders (*clientes*), who received gifts in return for their daily display of deference.

Along Via di Stabia. In the foreground, Italic atrium house with shop and thermopolium

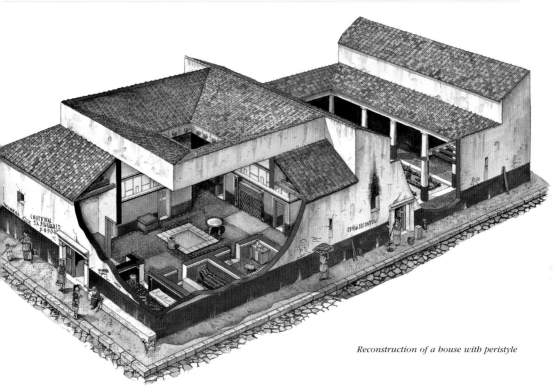

Reconstruction of a house with peristyle

THE HELLENISTIC HOUSE AND THE COUNTRY VILLA

During the 2nd century B.C., the growth of Roman hegemony in the Greek world fuelled a desire in the ambitious Pompeian nobility to remodel their homes in line with the palaces of the Greek aristocracy. There was an extraordinary growth in house decoration and furnishings, with the addition of peristyles, and gardens ornamented with Greek works of art (usually copies of famous sculptures and paintings) as well as nymphaeums (grottoes) with ingenious water-play. Heating systems were installed and the floors and walls were covered in decorations. Rather than inventing new architectural designs, the wealthy Pompeiians chose to renovate the traditional structure of the Italic house, making the appropriate modifications. They increased the number of rooms, or the size of the "modules", to create very large homes, further extended by integrating pre-existing complexes.

Furniture

Movable furniture was relatively rare, given that the beds, tables and cupboards were often built-in, and home-owners preferred to display their wall paintings in full view. The most important item of furniture was the bed, either for sleeping (*lectus cubicularis*) or for eating (*lectus tricliniaris*). In both cases, it could be embellished with decorations or other elements, finely worked in bronze or silver. There were usually three of the dining couches, arranged in a U-shape around a central table (*mensa*), made of marble, bronze or wood, which bore the household treasures. The dishes were placed on a larger table, generally rectangular. Similar care was taken over the positioning of the chairs, whose form and decoration related to the rank of the person seated. The cupboards were made of wood, and arranged in various places around the house. Sets of shelves and coffers, for example, might be displayed in the atrium if someone important was visiting, especially if they were finely decorated or reinforced like safes to conserve valuable objects. One of the most important articles for women was the "cista", a precious box for toiletries made from finely-worked bronze.

The garden

The place where the most radical changes took place was the area at the back of the house. Here, the traditional kitchen plot was replaced by an ornamental garden (*viridarium*), which could be very large in size. Using the framework of Hellenistic design, a variety of clever devices were employed to transform the walled area into a sort of earthly paradise. Thanks to the construction of the aqueduct in the Augustan era, which guaranteed a continuous, high-pressure supply, it was possible to create channels (*euripi*) which, by means of a complicated system could then feed water into pools, fountains and nymphaeans. The fortunate householder could cultivate his passion for "*otium*" (leisure), or take his meals outside in the "triclinium" (dining area). Rows of evergreen plants were flanked by medicinal herbs, and flowers and small fruit trees stood out against a background of fantastic scenes cleverly painted to create amazing illusions. These could depict natural scenes to expand the existing green space, or to compensate for a lack of it. They showed the imagined landscape of the Nile with scenes of pygmies hunting, while rows of columns helped create the impression of villas situated in won-

House of the Labyrinth, with tetrastyle atrium and peristyle

derful positions with views of the sea, harbours and ships, and scenes of hunting and fishing. The proprietor could sit in his enchanting garden and imagine he lived in the best of all possible worlds.

POMPEIAN PAINTING

Pompeian painting provides us with a unique overview of the development of Roman art between the 2nd century B.C. and 79 A.D. Not only can it be appreciated for its artistic value, but it also documents life at that period in an indispensable way, and provides us with important information about the Greco-Hellenistic style of painting, from which it chiefly derives. To categorize the differences between the surviving paintings, a classification system was developed known as the "Four Styles", useful in defining the chronology.

First style

This corresponds to the time from the maximum flourishing of the Samnite community to the establishment of the colony by Sulla, or from 200 B.C. to 80 B.C. It is also known as the "structural" style, in that it imitated the coloured veneer, marble or fine stone of the external walls of Hellenistic houses. It made great use of painted plaster to mimic architectural features. Some of the most important examples are found in the House of the Faun.

Second Style

This covers the period from the founding of the colony by Sulla to the early years of the reign of Augustus (from about 80 B.C. to 20 B.C.). It can partly be seen as an evolution of the First Style, with painting substituting for plaster. However, there is a new originality in the introduction of architectural elements, arranged to create spectacular (even if not always realistic) perspectives. Daring architectural images suddenly appear through painted windows, opening up a series of different depths.

From the Villa of the Mysteries, painting in second style

Sometimes these are explicit illusions, probably inspired by theatrical settings, or borrowed from the dynamic style of Hellenistic architecture.

At the same time, there is an extensive use of grandiose compositions, with the creation of large figurative friezes, the most famous example being in the Villa of the Mysteries. In this case, the emphasis is not on perspective and illusion but rather on recapturing some well-known examples of famous Greek art.

Third Style

This corresponded to the period from the reign of Augustus to that of Claudius (end of the 1st century B.C. to middle of the 1st century A.D.). Illusionistic devices had by now disappeared and were replaced by pictorial compositions with some abstract elements. They were delicately painted and imaginative, and provided a very elegant form of decoration. The centre of

From the House of the Vettii, an example of painting in fourth style

the wall, subdivided into three horizontal sections, often depicted a mythological tableau or an idyllic, sacred scene, framed between elegant panels decorated with architectural elements, plants or ornamental motifs, all painted with great finesse and an expert use of colour. Some well-preserved examples are found in the houses of Caecilius Jucundus and Marcus Lucretius Fronto.

Fourth Style

This is the most prominent in Pompeii, as it was still the current fashion at the time of the eruption. In many of the houses damaged by the earthquake, the earlier decorations were in the process of being replaced by up-to-date alternatives. The wall was still sub-divided into three sections, but this time elements of perspective were reintroduced, although not with the intention of creating optical illusions, but of expressing lively imagination and decorative skill.

VIEW OF THE CITY IN 79 A.D.

LEGEND:

1 *Villa of the Mysteries* **2** *Villa of Diomedes* **3** *Necropolis of Herculaneum Gate* **4** *Suburban Baths* **5** *Via dell'Abbondanza*
6 *Forum* **7** *Basilica* **8** *Temple of Jupiter* **9** *Macellum* **10** *Forum Baths* **11** *Stabian Baths* **12** *Temple of Isis*
13 *Large Theatre* **14** *Small Theatre/Odeon* **15** *House of Menander* **16** *Fullonicum of Stephanus* **17** *House of Octavius Quartio*
18 *House of Venus in the Shell* **19** *Amphitheatre* **20** *Large Palestra* **21** *Garden of the Fugitives*
22 *Lupanar* **23** *House of the Faun* **24** *House of the Vettii* **25** *House of the Small Fountain*

Necropolises: the Street of the Tombs

The law of the Twelve Tables, the first written legislation passed by the Roman Republic (about 450 B.C.), forbade any burial within the sacred confines of the pomerium, the legendary furrow ploughed by Romulus at the time the city was founded. The necropolises were therefore sited along the main roads leading into the town.

The Romans practised two kinds of burial: inhumation, with the body placed fully clothed and scattered with oils inside a sarcophagus; and incineration, involving ritual cremation of the dead and collection of the ashes in an urn, to be placed in a niche in the funerary monument.

The various tombs (including monumental stone sepulchres, small shrines, enclosures, memorial stones and altars), embellished with inscriptions, bas-reliefs and sometimes statues, become denser and denser approaching the city. In general, each one was owned by a family and equipped with a garden, a well for water and a *triclinium* for celebrating a meal with the dead on the anniversary of their death. It was also often furnished with a semi-circular seat (*schola*) for visitors to rest on.

The most important necropolis, in use in the first half of the 1st century B.C., is situated outside Herculaneum Gate, along the road leading from Naples. The first tomb, with a niche bearing a stone portrait, belonged to the Augustale (official of the cult of Augustus) Marcus Cerrinius Restitutus. Behind the *schola* of the priestess Mamia, there is a circular aedicule surmounting the large mausoleum of the rich Istacidi family, with statues of its members arranged between the columns. Further on, you come to the so-called Villa of Cicero, with mosaic columns and then a long arcade, behind which is a line of taverns. The tombs at the fork of the road are examples of the most recent type: a structure in the form of an altar raised on a tall marble base and surrounded by a low wall with bas-reliefs illustrating scenes from the life of the deceased. Some of the most interesting relate to the Augustale named Calventius, and display his special *bisellium* (double seat) in the first row of the theatre. Also of interest are the scenes on the tombs of Nevoleia Tyche and the Augustale Caius Munatius Faustus, where there is a depiction of a ship: the symbol of their mercantile activity, or of the journey of the soul of the deceased.

Street of the Tombs, tomb of the Augustale M. Cerrinius Restitutus. In the background, Herculaneum Gate

THE SUBURBAN BATHS

The bath complexes are among the most distinctive features of the Roman town. They were designed to satisfy that desire for pleasure (a blend of cultured conversation and *otium*) which constituted the main Roman contribution to the Hellenic concept of physical education: regarded as essential for the development of the individual. The Greek model, which viewed the baths as secondary in importance to the *palaestra* (gym), was therefore modified, and physical exercise became essentially a way to prepare the body for the delights of the bath. This evolutionary process can be clearly seen at Pompeii by looking at the successive bath complexes: from the Stabian Baths of the Samnite era, to the Forum Baths, built after the founding of the colony, to the more modern installations of the Central Baths and the Suburban Baths, under construction at the time of the eruption.

The Suburban Baths, just outside Marina Gate, date from the time of Augustus and are characterized by a lack of division between the sexes. After the changing-room (*apodyterium*), the various rooms are arranged in the traditional order of: the *frigidarium*, with cold water bath; the *tepidarium* with lukewarm bath; a small *laconicum* for high temperature sweat baths, and the *calidarium* for hot baths, built with an apse and large windows to make it more practical. The later addition of a large heated swimming-pool demonstrates the growing importance of this type of structure in city life.

Amongst the most striking decorative elements are the multi-coloured mosaic fountain, the paintings of sea-life, and the erotic pictures in the changing-room. Here, under each scene a numbered wooden box is painted, corresponding to those in which clothes were placed. The pictures have an explicit and unsophisticated immediacy, and it is not clear whether they were intended to suggest the presence of a brothel on the upper floor (to avoid sanctions or prohibitions which would have deprived the proprietors of certain civil rights), or whether they were simply a form of advertising.

Suburban Baths. In the background, Marina Gate

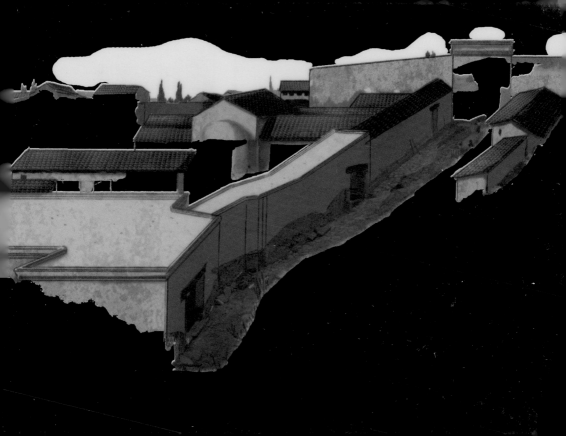

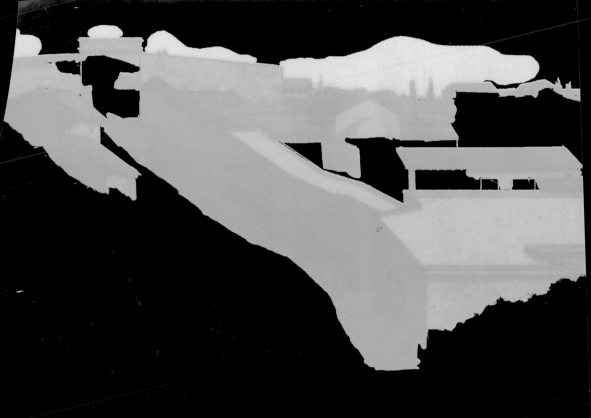

WALLS AND GATES

The pre-Roman walls in Pompeii are one of the most important surviving Italic defence systems. Even though the entire length of the wall has not been uncovered, we know that the perimeter followed the borders of the old lava deposit on which the city was built. This system of walls influenced the boundaries of the city, making it irregular in shape. The walls stretch for about 3200 metres, enclosing an area of about 66 hectares. The first defensive circle, made from lava blocks, was built at the beginning of the 6th century B.C., when the Auruncians held control of the area. Later, the fortifications were reinforced by the Samnites, at the time of the conflict with Rome and the war against Hannibal. This was done through the technique of the double wall in limestone blocks, the addition of an agger (rampart) and of a patrol path. At the time of the Social War, impor-

tant reinforcement work was carried out and new structures were built (including 13 towers) to prevent war machines from approaching the city. With the founding of the colony by Sulla, the need for defences declined. Public buildings and private homes were being put up on the other side of the walls, spilling down the hillside to enjoy a view of the sea, which then lay quite close to the city. The changes to the landscape can be seen at the Marina Gate, where the erection of the Suburban Baths and other buildings almost eliminated the walls and made the double-arched gate unrecognizable.

Herculaneum Gate, dating back to a restoration of the Roman period, had no explicit defensive purpose, while Nocera Gate, situated close to an important necropolis, dates back to the first phase of Samnite control. Another necropolis can be found outside Nola Gate.

At the end of Via di Mercurio, tower and walls

THE ROADS

The system of roads in Pompeii reflects the historic development of the city. The narrowest and winding streets typify the old centre grown up around the Forum, while the recent districts exhibit a planning system hinging on the axes of two "*decumani*" (main streets), intersected at regular distances by "*cardi*" (streets running north-south) as to create equally-sized blocks. Each of them could contain a collection of dwellings, a large mansion or a public building. The width of the streets reached a maximum in the decuman known as Via dell'Abbondanza and in the main cardo named Via di Stabia. The carriageway was composed of many-sided flagstones, with the inclusion of raised blocks to enable pedestrians to cross in times of heavy rain or in the presence of waste water (as there was no proper drainage system). The holes in the pavements may have been designed to hold poles for supporting the stalls. Many crossroads were equipped with public fountains, supplied by the Augustan aqueduct – the *castellum aquae* (water cistern) was near Vesuvius Gate – via a system of water towers and lead pipes. The main streets, lined with shops, taverns, and *thermopolia* (food stalls), were thronged with merchants, shopkeepers, artisans, clients and idlers, while along the carriageway passed light horse-drawn carriages, heavy two-wheeled carts pulled by mules or oxen, and litters for the wealthier citizens. There were also soothsayers, musicians, jugglers and beggars...

Certain areas, like the Forum and the residential streets, were closed of with stones insurmountable by vehicles, and others were one-way. On the still visible deep ruts, caused by the passage of heavy wheels, were addressed the means of transport.

*Via del Foro with the arch next to the rear
of the Temple of Jupiter. In the background, the Forum*

Fountain and thermopolium at the crossroads between Via Consolare and Via di Modesto

THE FORUM

The Forum, crowded and animated, was the true heart of city life. It was surrounded by the administrative buildings, temples and monuments to historic events or myths which constituted the essential structure of *civitas* (citizenship), making it the most prestigious and imposing place in the city. It was used for meetings, business, discussions, politics, public demonstrations, exchanges of every type, study and leisure.

During the 2nd century B.C., the old market square of the Samnite town was made grander in line with the Hellenistic-Roman model, becoming a long rectangular area surrounded by a portico with two rows of tuff columns. The main focus was the Temple of Jupiter, framed by two triumphal arches with statues of the emperors in niches, and opposite this stood the offices of public administration. The other buildings were arranged along the two sides: to the west was the monumental basilica, the Temple of Apollo and the Forum Holitorium (the market for vegetables and cereals) with adjacent latrines. On the opposite side stood the large Macellum (the meat and fish market), preceded by a row of shops. Other structures, erected in the imperial age after the original shops had been demolished, reflected the new ideology of the rulers: the so-called Sanctuary of the Public Lares was dedicated to the cult of the emperor, and the Temple of Vespasian was devoted to the Genius of Augustus. The imposing Building of Eumachia, a magnificent example of private patronage, may have served as a wool exchange. At the centre of the square was a basement for an equestrian statue of Augustus, while on the west side and in front of the administrative buildings stood many statues (some equestrian) dedicated to members of the imperial family or to prominent citizens.

Porticoes on the west side of the Forum

TEMPLE OF APOLLO, FORUM HOLITORIUM AND LATRINES

Some fragments remain of the original temple, established at the beginning of the 6th century B.C. However, the building in its current form dates from the 2nd century B.C. and was the most important cultural building in the city, strategically located at the intersection of two main streets.

The temple was enclosed by a monumental colonnade, creating a very impressive spectacle. The Hellenistic design shows the influence of Rome's eastern territories. However, the cella (*sanctum*), raised on a high podium with steps to the front, is still essentially Italic in style.

After the earthquake in 62 A.D., restoration work was begun, and was still in progress at the time of the eruption. It was aimed at adapting the building in line with the taste for precious materials which typified the imperial age. The columns were covered in stucco to imitate marble, their capitals were transformed to the Corinthian style, and the entrances to the Forum were closed off. The large altar, on the other hand, had been added previously. Inside could be seen the statue of the cult and the tuff *omphalos*, an attribute of Apollo at Delphi, considered as the navel of the world. The two bronze statues of Apollo and Diana with her bow are copies of the originals now kept at the Archaeological Museum in Naples.

In a niche in the east wall of the temple can be found the "Mensa Ponderaria" (official measuring table) of the Forum Holitorium of Oscan origin, as the original names for the measures show: still visible is the large limestone slab containing nine cavities of various sizes, each with a hole at the bottom to allow the product to be extracted once the measurement had been made.

The next portico, with eight brick pillars, marks the entrance to the Forum Holitorium, the market for vegetables and cereals, which was also not completed at the time of the eruption. The nearby latrine was one of the latest innovations: it consisted of three seats arranged in a U-shape, with a drainage channel underneath.

THE BASILICA

The Basilica is the most important civil building in Pompeii. It faces onto the south-west corner of the Forum with one of its short sides, contrary to the usual custom with this type of building. Christian basilicas based on this model also adopted the same arrangement. Its structure mimics that of the Forum, but in a more organic and finished way. It was built in about 130-120 B.C., as part of a huge rebuilding programme in Pompeii, and was used to administer civil and commercial law and to draw up financial and trading agreements.

There were five doors giving access to the Basilica, sheltered by an imposing portico. The building is laid out in the form of a large rectangle measuring 55 x 24 metres, and divided into three naves by 28 huge brick columns. These supported the strong wooden framework of the pitched roof, braced by half-columns in the side naves. Light could only enter the building through breaches in the inter-columniations. The *tribunal* (whose exact function is still debated), stands against the back wall: it has been partially restored using original pieces. It consists of an imposing façade with two orders of columns, Corinthian and Ionic, raised on a podium over two metres high and surmounted by an imposing tympanum: a design inspired by the Hellenistic buildings of Pergamum. The lack of any fixed means of access has led to the idea that the podium was reserved for magistrates, who might have climbed up to it using movable wooden stairs, to ensure their protection in violent disputes. According to another hypothesis, the platform could have served as a *sacellum* (votive chapel for statues of the cult, and trials would then have taken place in the two side aisles, accessible from the central room. The building was decorated in plaster painted in the first style (false stones), and the columns were coated with white plaster.

THE BUILDING OF EUMACHIA

The inscription on the architrave celebrates the woman who financed this building, constructed between 14 and 37 A.D. Her name was Eumachia, Priestess of Venus, and she ordered it to be built "in her own name and that of her son", dedicating it to *Concordia* and *Pietas Augusta.* The words *Concordia* and *Pietas* allude to the agreement between Livia and Tiberius, heir to the *imperator,* following Augustus's death. The parallel between Eumachia and her son and the imperial family indicates the loyalty of noble Pompeians to the new order instituted by Augustus. This celebration of the imperial house was emphasized by the statues placed in niches on the façade of the Forum, and reinforced by inscriptions which lauded the venerable ancestors of the *gens Iulia* by means of the cult of Romulus and Aeneas.

The entranceway was rebuilt after the earthquake of 62 A.D. The frieze surrounding it is an example of the Augustan style, and may have been taken from the Temple of Vespasian. To the sides of the entrance are two niches, which were probably used by auctioneers to conduct sales and which indicate the commercial use of the building. The interior consists of a large colonnaded rectangle, with covered shops along the longer sides. The enormous apse opposite the entrance, flanked by two side apses, housed the Statue of Concordia, while in the covered corridor behind there was a statue dedicated to Eumachia by the association of *fullones* (wool processors). In a room to the right of the entrance, there stood a large jar containing urine for de-greasing the wool, which was treated in an open area, using vats, laundries and tanks.

The Building of Eumachia, entranceway and interior

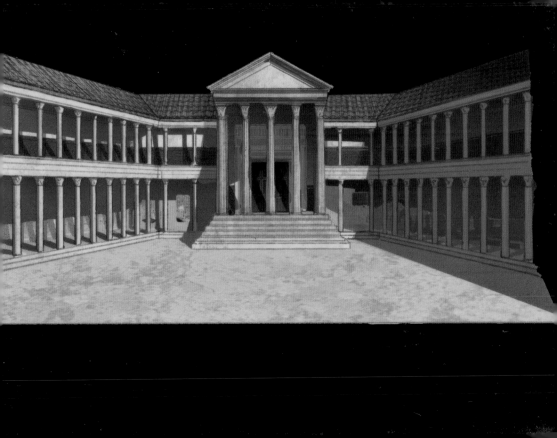

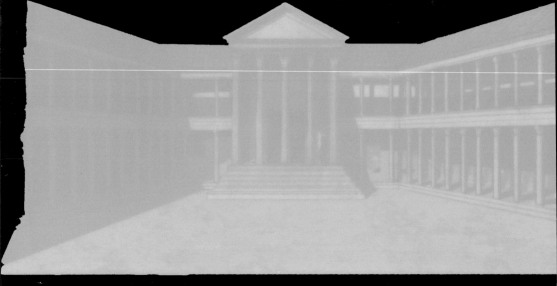

TEMPLE OF VESPASIAN AND SANCTUARY OF THE LARES

The Temple attributed to Vespasian was more likely dedicated to the cult of Augustus and was presumably built during the Augustan age or immediately after it, possibly at the expense of the Priestess Mamia. It consists of a large colonnaded courtyard, still being restored after the earthquake, which was originally preceded by a façade with four columns. A cella stood against the wall at the back. The most interesting feature is the sacrificial altar, made of marble and standing on a low plinth, decorated with elegant bas-reliefs. This object escaped the process of retrieving marble items following the eruption, which led to the disappearance of nearly all the precious materials in the Forum. On the side facing the entrance, a scene shows the sacrifice of a bull, with a small tetrastyle temple in the background: possibly the very one which houses the altar, in which case the relief might be depicting its inauguration. The figure on the left with the

veiled head is the priest, who is intent on pouring libations onto a tripod. He is flanked by lictors while opposite him stands the *victimarius* (executioner) armed with the ritual axe. The short side of the altar portray the ceremonial instruments while the side facing the *cella* shows a crown of oak leaves, the emblem of imperial authority. The magnificent ornamentation, visible on the portal, may once have formed part of the decoration of the temple. The *sacellum* dedicated to the Public Lares, to which the fate of the city were entrusted, consists of a spacious court open to the sky with a large apse at the far end. The building was probably built after the earthquake of 62 A.D. as a sign of expiation to placate the fury of the gods. The image of the Public Lares would therefore have been positioned in the large apse, flanked by statues of other divinities. An alternative theory suggests that the sanctuary was dedicated to the cult of the imperial family.

The altar of the Temple of Vespasian in the Forum

THE MACELLUM

The Macellum is an imposing building, in Hellenistic and Punic design, where meat and fish were sold. Probably built in the 2nd century B.C., it was placed in a slightly withdrawn position so as not to interfere with the life of the Forum. It was restructured at the time of the Julio-Claudian dynasty, and was undergoing restoration at the time of the eruption. There were three entrances to the market: a secondary entrance in the south-east corner; another on the south side, flanked by a row of shops, and the main entrance on the west side, with a line of shops of decreasing size. Three marble columns remain here, together with bases for statues. This entrance is divided into two parts by an aedicule. The internal space was surrounded by a colonnade, and in its centre stood a basin of water sheltered by a twelve-sided *tholos* (circu-

The northeastern arcade of the Forum and the shops in front of the Macellum

lar building), whose conical roof was supported by wooden poles anchored in stone bases. The *sacellum* at the back was probably dedicated to the imperial cult. The two statues of a priestess and of a man with naked torso standing in a heroic pose (the originals are in the Archaeological Museum in Naples) are thought to represent members of the imperial family or local patrons who financed the reconstruction work. A room on the east side, adorned with a small altar, was probably used for sacrificial banquets in honour of the emperor. Another room to the right of this, containing sloping stone counters and a waste water channel, was used for the sale of fish. Along the west and north walls can be seen the remains of some fine decoration in the fourth style, with small paintings of mythological subjects and still life panels.

The entrance to the Macellum; the aedicule with the capitals decorated with chimeras from the Tomb of the Garlands. In the foreground, the columns of the Forum

THE TEMPLE OF JUPITER

The temple stands in a dominating position at the end of the Forum and originally was probably only dedicated to Jupiter, whose cult was very widespread amongst the Italic people. It was only after the establishment of the Sullan colony that it came to be dedicated to Jupiter, Juno and Minerva, the Capitoline Triad honored in Rome.

The original structure, raised on a high podium, was built in the 2nd century B.C. and conforms to the Etrusco-Italic tradition. The particular attention lavished on the Temple of Jupiter, which was constantly embellished during the imperial age and was still being reconstructed in 79 A.D., attests to the great political and religious significance of the building, and so the loyalty of Pompeii to the Roman world and its ideals. The pronaos was extremely deep, with six tuff columns at the front and four to the sides: adorned with Corinthian capitals, they each measured about 12 metres in height and were coated in plaster. It probably dates back to the Tiberian epoch, when the altar, which was originally positioned in front of the steps in the centre of the Forum, was removed to a large platform in the middle of the staircase. This was rebuilt on a larger scale to accommodate the new structure, with a stairway on each side leading up to temple. The façade was adorned with two equestrian monuments. The cella was divided into three parts by two rows of Ionic columns, with upper sections in the Corinthian style. At the back, raised on another podium, was the three-part aedicule dedicated to the Capitoline Triad. The surviving decorations are amongst the most interesting examples of the third style. Inside the podium are some vaulted rooms, divided into three aisles to support the structure above. These may have served as a *favissa* (depository for sacred objects) or as an *aerarium* (public treasury).

Forum and Temple of Jupiter with the arch, at the beginning of Via di Mercurio, and Arch of Caligula in the background. Another honorary arch on the left of the temple

THE FORUM BATHS

The complex was financed with public money at the time of the Sullan colony, and is smaller in size than the older Stabian Baths. Clients paid a modest price to enter the baths, but extra for such services as massages and custody of clothes. The baths stayed open until after sunset, with lighting provided by lamps. The male section was separated from the female part by the *praefurnium*, and women had no access to the *palaestra*. The men's baths could be accessed from Via del Foro, Vicolo delle Terme and Via delle Terme. The first two entrances opened into a small courtyard surrounded by columns, which led into the *apodyterium*. This room contained masonry benches and wooden shelves for clothes, and had yellow-painted walls and a decorated vault. Light came from an overhead skylight. The *frigidarium* consisted of a small, round room with a domed ceiling and skylight and a raised tub in the centre. The room was painted in red, blue and yellow and featured stucco decorations with cupids. The *tepidarium* was heated by a bronze brazier instead of the modern system of under-floor heating, which could perhaps have been destroyed in the earthquake. Some of the stucco decoration survived. The telamons (supporting figures) positioned between the niches used for oil, perfume and bathroom objects, have been attributed to the earliest period of the building. The vaulted ceiling also has skylights and the opulent decoration here was added after the 62 A.D. earthquake. The calidarium is very well preserved and equipped with a modern heating system. The walls are painted a golden yellow, with red pilasters supporting a cornice from which rises the barrel vault. The apse contains the *labrum* (cold water bath).

Frigidarium *of the Forum Baths*

Calidarium *of the Forum Baths*

THE STABIAN BATHS

The small tubs located in the north-west corner of the *palaestra* date back to the 4th century B.C. and are the oldest thermal plant in Pompeii which is still visible today. The structure became a public bath and was extended in the 2nd century B.C., being divided into two sections served by the same furnaces. Further modernization was carried out in the early years of the Roman colony. The main entrance leads into a trapezium-shaped *pal-*

Palaestra *of the Stabian Baths*

aestra, colonnaded on three sides in the style of the time. The shafts of the columns were coated with plaster in the years after the earthquake. The large latrine and the pool, flanked by two rooms used for washing feet, date back to the middle of the 1st century B.C. The west side of the *palaestra* is embellished with rich stucco decoration in the fourth style, depicting imaginary architecture and figures of gods and heroes.

Similar rich decorations in multi-coloured stucco can also be seen in the vestibule and probably date from after 62 A.D. The *apodyterium* is also striking: the decoration here is similar to that in the Forum Baths but even more sumptuous. The *frigidarium* contains the typical round bath with steps. The paintings showing gardens and the starry scene on the dome have virtually disappeared. The *tepidarium* and *calidarium*, undergoing reconstruction in 79 A.D., contain a very modern heating system. The floor raised on small brick pillars (*hypocaustum*) allowed the passage of hot air, which then circulated by means of pipes inserted in the walls. The women's section was similar to the men's but more simply decorated.

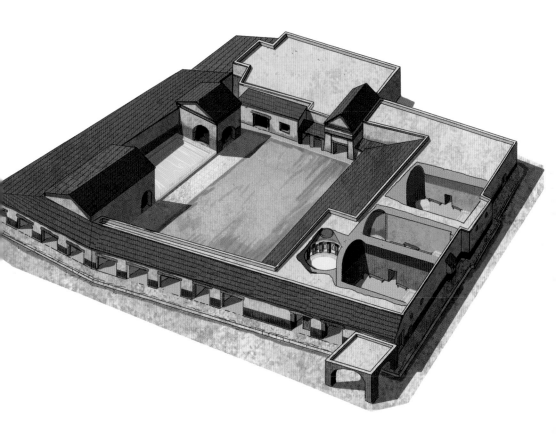

THE TRIANGULAR FORUM, THE DORIC TEMPLE, THE SAMNITE PALAESTRA AND THE TEMPLE OF ISIS

The Triangular Forum stands on top of a spur of lava perched high above the plain. The view from here is so splendid that during the period of reconstruction following the earthquake the area between here and the sea was left free of buildings. The present state of the forum dates from the middle of the 2nd century B.C., when the entrance portico with six columns was erected. A grand colonnade was also constructed to enhance the Doric Temple, first established in the 6th century B.C. and remodelled many times. Now only the base of it survives. Just south of the temple is a *tholos*, probably originally covered by a conical roof, which served to protect a well.

On the north-east side, there is access to the Samnite *Palaestra*, dating from the 2nd century B.C. This was reduced in size after the 62 A.D. earthquake to make more room for the Temple of Isis, the focus of a widespread cult in relation to the famous "mysteries". The original temple, raised on a podium, was built out of tuff towards the end of the 2nd century B.C. and reconstructed in brickwork following the earthquake. It stands inside a small Corinthian portico which housed the living quarters of the priests and some altars. A small enclosure in the south-east corner descended in a basement where the sacred waters of the Nile were kept for the purification ceremonies. A staircase gave access to the *pronaos* (porch) supported by four columns at the front and two at the sides. Niches at the back held statues of Harpokrates and Anubis, associated with the cult of Isis. At the rear of the cella was the base for a statue. The lively architecture was complemented by exuberant stucco decorations and very sophisticated pictures depicting still life, Trojan scenes, naval battles and Egyptian landscapes: all now in the Naples Archaeological Museum.

Temple of Isis

THE LARGE THEATRE AND THE QUADRIPORTICUS

The Large Theatre was built in the 2nd century B.C., on the same lava plinth as the Doric Temple, and could seat 5000. Although it underwent restoration in the Augustan era, it still maintains its essential Greek structure. The *cavea* (auditorium), originally separated from the stage, was in the shape of a horse-shoe, and the steps followed the natural slope of the hillside. The lower part of the auditorium (*ima cavea*), nearest to the stage and containing the widest seats, was overlaid with

Quadriporticus, transformed into barracks for gladiators after 62 A.D.

marble and reserved for important personages. The *media cavea* (middle section) was used by representatives of artisan associations and prominent citizens. The seats above the entrance corridors (*parodoi*), originally uncovered, were reserved for city officials and date from the time of Augustus. The same was true of the circular corridor supporting the highest seats (*summa cavea*), used by the other spectators and by women. The front of the stage rested on the walls of the *parodoi*, where the holes which held the supporting beams for the curtain are still visible. The stage consisted of a central apse flanked by two rectangular niches. The performances included Greek dramas, adapted to Roman tastes, and new genres such as the *fabula atellana*, a plebeian style of farce. Mimed entertainment was also popular, featuring actors and actresses who would undress at the audience's request. Later, a form of pantomime was introduced, with the actors miming mythological events to the accompaniment of music. Behind the theatre was a large quadriporticus which served as a foyer, a typical feature of the Greek style theatre. It was later transformed into barracks for gladiators, signalling the end of the concept of a Greek theatre.

THE ODEON (OR SMALL THEATRE) AND THE TEMPLE OF ASCLEPIUS

The Odeon, built next to the Large Theatre in the early years of the Sullan colony, forms with it a single complex. It was constructed. We know that the theatre was roofed to enhance the acoustics for musical entertainment and poetic recitals. To help support the roof, the wings of the auditorium were truncated at the edges in a straight line. The theatre had a capacity of about 1500-2000 seats and, according to a recent theory, would have been reserved for those settlers who did not speak Osco: the language used in shows at the Large Theatre, and at political meetings. The seating divisions were similar to those in the Large Theatre. However, it differed from that in terms of the size and form of the orchestra, which in this case was circular, with a balustrade separating off the *ima cavea*. The low and wide steps in this section, decorated with the feet of winged griffons, were designed to accommodate the *bisel-*

A detail of the Odeon or Small Theatre

lia: luxury chairs reserved for the decurions. The *media cavea* was divided into five wedges, and ended with tuff sculptures of kneeling telamons which supported the side walls of the *parodoi*. The floor of the orchestra was decorated with coloured marble slabs and dates from the first Augustan period. The stage was fitted with a curtain and with three doors, which led off it to the "changing rooms".

The Temple of Asclepius, also known as the Temple of Jupiter Meilichios, dates from the 2nd century B.C. and was entered from Via di Stabia. A portico with two columns led into a courtyard, in the centre of which stood an altar covered with tuff slabs and decorated with a Doric frieze. The cella on a podium was preceded by a staircase which gave access to a tetrastyle *pronaos* in the Corinthian style. Inside the cella, you can still see the bases of statues, possibly those of Asclepius and Hygea.

The Odeon or Small Theatre

THE HOUSE OF MENANDER

The immense size of the house (the floor area measures more than 1800 square metres) has led to the conclusion that it was probably owned by important representatives of Pompeii's governing class, possibly the family of Poppaeus, related to Poppea, wife of Nero. The original layout of the atrium, dating from the 3rd century B.C., underwent a huge transformation a century later. With the demolition of some neighbouring houses, a series of new rooms were created, such as a peristyle, bath area, kitchen and servants' quarters. Following these operations, the central focus of the house shifted from the atrium to the garden with peristyle, around which the most luxurious rooms were arranged. The benches still visible in front of the house were used by people waiting to call on the owner. In the atrium with *impluvium*, richly decorated in the fourth style, is a large temple-style *lararium*, next to which a stone staircase provides access to the upper floor. The surrounding rooms are decorated with magnificent pictures including episodes from the Trojan War, as well as a fine *emblema* (a high quality mosaic made with very small tiles) showing a Nilotic scene and typical of the 1st or 2nd style. In the peristyle, you can still see a painting portraying the playwright Menander. To the right of this, there was another religious shrine designed to hold the *imagines maiorum*: the wooden busts or wax masks representing the ancestors.

The nearby bath complex was built around a tetrastyle courtyard, and was in the process of restoration in 79 A.D. The *calidarium* is decorated with a mosaic floor showing figures of Nubians swimming among fish. A famous silver treasure was discovered in the cellars, consisting of a fine 118-piece table service. This had been carefully stored in a wooden chest which also contained (in a smaller casket) some pieces of gold jewellery and a large collection of coins.

The atrium of the House of Menander

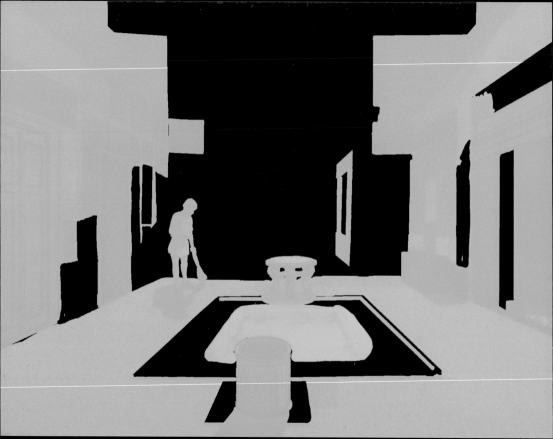

THE INSCRIPTIONS ON THE WALLS

As you walk along the streets of Pompeii, and in particular Via dell'Abbondanza, your attention is inevitably drawn to the large inscriptions in red and black letters which stand out clearly on the faces of both public and private buildings, shops, and even on the walls of funereal monuments. These inscriptions, which were found in great numbers during the course of excavations, date back to the period between the last phase of Samnite rule in Pompeii (end of the 2nd century B.C.) and the moment of the city's destruction. They relate to a variety of subjects: administrative acts, rental notices, programmes for festivals and public ceremonies, publicity for shows, moral maxims, messages of love, tributes to theatrical personalities, praise for the exploits (especially amatory) of gladiators, advertisements for services offered by prostitutes, protestations of thanks for favours granted by the emperor, information about different types of foodstuff, and so on. The most common category, however, was that of the so-called electoral announcements. The city magistrates were elected every year and their supporters (relatives, friends or professional associations) put considerable effort into preparing a section of wall with white plaster, perhaps covering over the previous year's inscription, and putting up their various election demands. There was never mention of any programme: generally, the notice gave the name of the candidate (so called because anyone running for public office would wear a white "candida" toga), followed by the office he aspired to and an exhortation to vote for him. This message was often abbreviated to single initials, such as OVF (*Oro Vos Faciat*: "please do it", i.e. vote), while the candidate's supposed qualities could be condensed into two letters such as VB (*Vir Bonum*, "man for the good"), perhaps accompanied by abuse against anyone daring to cancel the inscription: "May he be carried off by disease!"

An electoral announcement on the walls of Pompeii

THE THERMOPOLIUM OF L. VETUTIUS PLACIDUS

Most of the town's population, and not just the less prosperous, would eat meals at one of the many open-air food stalls. Lunch was generally a frugal meal even for the well-to-do, and it was usual to eat in the street while going about one's business. It is estimated that there were at least two hundred places in Pompeii (*tabernae, thermopolia, popinae and cauponae*) where one could eat a quick meal either standing up or sitting down. These food stalls are easily recognisable by their built-in counters in which were set a number of large amphorae containing the food or drink for sale. You could order cold drinks or mulled wine and eat such delicacies as olives, fish in brine, pieces of roast meat, birds on a skewer, stewed octopus, fruit, sweets and cheese. The less well-off, who lived in rented accommodation and did not have cooking facilities, would often bring their food here to be heated up. Like the other shops, the *thermopolia* (food stalls) faced onto the street and had a wide opening with a threshold. This entrance was closed off at night by means of a sliding wooden door with hinged sections.

The *thermopolium* of Vetutius Placidus on Via dell'Abbondanza was identified as such by the inscriptions painted on the façade and those on some of the amphorae found in the garden. It was one of the largest in the town, with a three-sided counter in polychrome marble and stucco, and equipped with an oven for preparing hot food and drinks. On one wall, is a painted *lararium*, depicting the Genius performing a sacrifice on a tripod, flanked by the Lares and by Mercury, messenger to the gods, and Dionysius, god of wine. The room at the back, possibly a *triclinium*, was used by customers who wanted to eat sitting down.

The Thermopolium of L. Vetutius Placidus

A thermopolium *along Via di Stabia*

THE FULLONICUM (FULLERY) OF STEPHANUS

The textile business was sustained by a flourishing sheep-rearing industry and by active trading of the finished product. However, the most important factor here was the important role that maintenance of one's wardrobe played in the economic life of the city. The social and legal status of men and women was recognized by the clothes they wore. Apart from suggesting your disposable income, your clothes could also indicate your status as freeman or slave, your social position and political role, and sometimes even your profession. Wool was used for making classic garments such as the male toga, and the women's stola and palla (dress and cloak). The wool was prepared in a series of workshops specializing in different stages of the process. In the *officinae lanifricariae*, the raw wool was first boiled and then beaten. It was then passed on to the *officinae textoriae*, to be spun and made into cloth before being finally sent to the *officinae tintoriae* to be dyed. In the *fullonica* (fulleries), the cloth received its final de-greasing prior to sale. These laundries also washed and removed stains from used garments to enable them to be re-worn. The Fullonicum of Stephanus, so called because of an electoral message inscribed on its façade, was created by modifying an original house with atrium. The *impluvium* bath was used for washing fine cloth; the flat roof (the only example in Pompeii) was probably used for drying it; the three oval baths in the peristyle were used for treading the cloth, using de-greasing substances such as urine. This urine, whether animal or human, was kept in special containers. The cloth was then treated with fuller's earth, beaten, and finally rinsed in the three large baths. The room alongside served as a kitchen for the workers.

The Fullonicum of Stephanus

HOUSE OF OCTAVIUS QUARTIO

This residence was once mistakenly thought to belong to Loreius Tiburtinus. Until the earthquake struck, it also included the neighbouring atrium-style dwelling, making it (with a surface area of 2700 square metres) one of the largest houses in the city to occupy an entire *insula* (block). At the front are two *cauponae* (taverns). These connect to the inside by means of a doorway, which also gives access to the upper floor. There is a bench by the entrance for waiting clients. The section of the house which includes the atrium was built in the 2nd century B.C. Subsequently, the *impluvium* here was transformed into a trough for ornamental plants, indicating how this section came to be regarded as less important than the large garden: very much the fashion at the time. Thanks to a careful programme of excavation and reclamation, which included making copies of the trees, it was possible to accurately recreate the garden, planting it with the original species and reconstructing the

wooden pergolas. The layout was designed around two water channels, known as "euripi", arranged in the shape of a "T". The first of these, lying parallel to the house, was connected to a *biclinium* (dining area) for open-air meals, embellished with a *nymphaeum* (grotto). It was decorated with pumice-stones, and surrounded with paintings by the artist Lucius depicting scenes from myths associated with water: Narcissus regarding his reflection at the spring and the story of Pyramus and Thisbe. A line of marble statues of animals, deities, sphinxes and muses faces onto the euripus, and, together with the paintings related to Isis in the south-west room, gives the whole area a peculiarly Egyptian atmosphere. The water passes through a *nymphaeum*, surmounted by a temple with columns, and then flows into the lower euripus. This canal is divided into a succession of basins with water fountains, and extends the whole width of the garden, facilitating irrigation of the fruit trees.

The garden of the House of Octavius Quartio

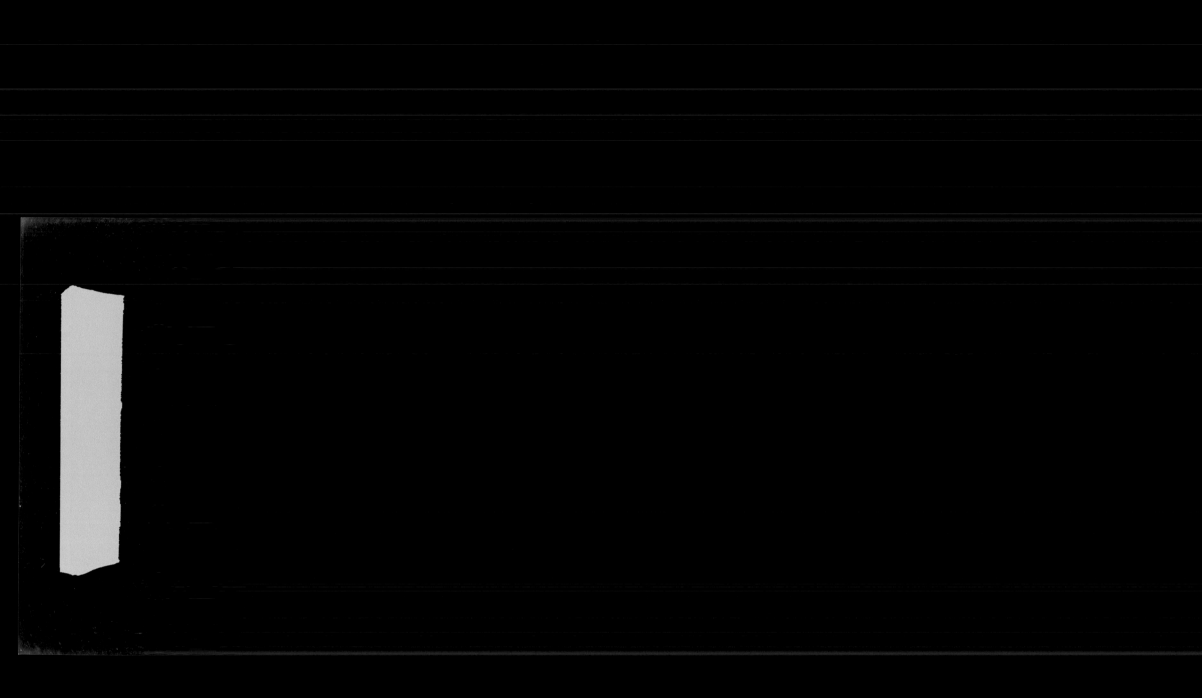

HOUSE OF VENUS IN THE SHELL AND HOUSE OF THE GARDEN OF HERCULES

Given its large size, this house must have belonged to a wealthy person. It appears to be the result of restructuring a typical atrium-style house, but sadly suffered bomb damage in 1943. The *tablinum* was sacrificed, possibly during the imperial age, in order to enlarge the peristyle behind it. The large *triclinium* opened both onto the atrium and onto the peristyle, enabling diners to enjoy the view of the garden. This room was undergoing restoration at the time of the eruption: indeed the plaster on the walls had just been roughly outlined. The *viri-*

Painting with Venus in the shell, along with two cupids

darium (garden) was the most important feature of the peristyle-type house, with all the main rooms gathered around it. The portico, with tall columns covered in gold and white plaster, extended along two sides of the peristyle, providing a screen for the living rooms. The southern wall, which was bare of columns, was entirely occupied by a large painted tableau. The lower part is taken up with a very realistic-looking hedge, and the side panels behind this depict a lush garden filled with flowering shrubs, herons, pheasants, and doves drinking from marble urns, plus a statue of Mars on a high pedestal. By contrast, the large central panel depicts a seascape, with Venus lying on a conch shell accompanied by two nymphs: they seem to be travelling towards the city placed under her protection. Before being extended to include a large garden, the House of the Hercules (or House of the Perfumer) was typical of that type of "terraced" house dating from the 3rd century B.C. Due to the modest size of the structure, the usual atrium was replaced by an open, rectangular courtyard, and the rooms were arranged along both sides of a long corridor ending in a small garden. The second floor may have been added at a later date.

Peristyle of the House of Venus in the Shell

THE AMPHITHEATRE

This is one of the oldest and best preserved amphitheatres. It dates from about 80 B.C., and was built by the same officials responsible for the creation of the Odeon. The building was completed thanks to contributions from the magistrates of both the city and the *pagus suburbanus* (rural area), and held 20,000 spectators. It was sited in an outlying area devoid of other buildings, to make use of the city walls to support the *cavea* and to facilitate the flow of spectators. The *cavea* rests on an artificial embankment surrounded by an oval wall with buttresses, characterized by a façade with blind arches. The entrance stairways were built up against the perimeter wall. This was not the custom with modern amphitheatres, where the entrance galleries were incorporated into the walls to let the audience easily in. The places for magistrates in the *ima cavea*, at a level below that of the

square, and the seats in the *media cavea*, could be accessed via a covered corridor entered by two passages on the western side. The upper gallery was probably reserved for women, in line with a decree by Augustus, separating them from the other spectators and from the arena. You can still see the large stone rings used to support the beams from which the linen *velarium* was hung to protect the audience from the sun. The two passageways to the north and south of the gallery led into the arena; while that on the west side was probably the entrance used by the magistrate presiding over the games. In 59 A.D., the famous brawl broke out between the Pompeians and the Nucerians, whose city had taken over part of the territory of Pompeii. This led to a ten-year ban on the use of the amphitheatre, lifted by Nero after the earthquake of 62 A.D.

The Amphitheatre seen from outside

The Amphitheatre

THE LARGE PALAESTRA AND THE NOCERA GATE NECROPOLIS

The Large Palaestra was constructed in the Augustan era, occupying an empty site to the west of the amphitheatre. The intention was to increase the *virtus* (worth) of the leading ranks in society by means of physical activity, in line with the imperial policy of glorifying the mystique of youth. The *palaestra* consisted of a large green area shaded by two rows of plane trees. It was bordered on three sides by a colonnade of 118 columns raised on a podium, and protected by high walls which were originally crenelated in imitation of a *castrum* (castle). A swimming pool was built in the centre. On the west side was a shrine probably dedicated to the cult of the Emperor, while the south portico gave access to a latrine. In the rooms on south side, the athletes could prepare themselves for their exercises, or clean themselves with strigils. The north wall, which became visible again as a result of modern restoration work, preserves traces of decorations in the third style. The *palaestra* could serve as a parade ground for training foot soldiers and cavalry. It could also serve as a place of shelter for spectators at the amphitheatre during bad weather; a destination for walks; a venue for teaching far from the chaos of the city; an area for cock-fighting; a market-place for slaves, and a barracks. The necropolis at Nocera Gate, used from the 1st century B.C., includes tombs of every type, although mainly in the style of the aedicule or exedra. Prominent amongst these is the tomb of Eumachia, sponsor of the building in the Forum. The tomb of the Flavii is notable for its structure, with a *fornix* (vault) introduced into the two burial chambers, and niches on the façade containing images of the deceased, as it was the custom amongst freedmen.

The Nocera Gate Necropolis

THE GLADIATORIAL GAMES

The Pompeians followed gladiatorial games with a fanaticism which could border on excess; as it did in that celebrated brawl of 59 A.D., which ended with many dead and wounded. The considerable cost of the games was borne by the magistrates, who often competed with each other to provide the most splendid spectacles. The season began in February and ended in July. The events lasted from 3 to 5 days and involved up to 35 pairs of gladiators. The expenses were high and large fortunes were dissipated in financing memorable contests. After the earthquake of 62 A.D., the gladiators were quartered in the quadriporticus (colonnaded quadrangle) of the Large Theatre, as is confirmed by the weapons and graffiti discovered there. Most of the gladiators were professionals (generally slaves) and were sold or hired to the directors of the schools in which they were trained. There were different types of combatants: for example, the *Thraex* (Tracian) was lightly armed with a round shield, short sword and a flashy helmet; the *Hoplomachus* wore heavy armour, while the *Retiarius* carried a net and a trident. The contests were ferocious and the spectators were often called upon to decide whether the loser should live or die. If it was a question of a skilled fighter or a free man, costly in financial terms and probably loved by the public, then the tendency was to spare him. The other spectacle, which often followed the gladiatorial contests, was the *venatio*, in which wild animals would fight between each other or with the gladiators. As the amphitheatre was not equipped with underground pens for holding the animals, they had to be transported in cages and released into the arena.

A type of gladiator: Myrmillo

The gladiators:
Secutor, Thraex, Retiarius

THE GARDEN OF THE FUGITIVES

The Garden of the Fugitives takes up a block previously occupied by houses which, in the last years of Pompeii, was transformed into a vineyard. This was equipped with a *triclinium* for outdoor eating during the summer months and masonry couches for relaxation. During the excavations conducted by Amadeo Maiuri in 1961, the bodies of 13 victims of the 79 A.D. eruption were discovered. These were the corpses of adults, youngsters and children, possibly from the same family groups. After remaining indoors for a while to avoid the rain of ashes and lava fragments, they then attempted to flee through Nocera Gate when the mass of volcanic debris threatened to overwhelm their house. This is how they died of suffocation in the middle of the garden.

Their bodies were revealed and conserved thanks to a technique developed in the nineteenth century by Fiorelli, the director of excavations at the time: "On February 5th 1863, while in the process of clearing an alleyway, Fiorelli was told by his workers that they had discovered a cavity, at the bottom of which they had noticed some bones. With a true stroke of genius, Fiorelli ordered the men to stop working and mix some plaster, which was then poured into this cavity and into two others nearby. After checking that the plaster was dry, they carefully removed the hard crust of pumice and ashes. When these casings were eliminated, the shapes of four corpses were revealed". These plaster casts were then replaced in the exact locations where they had been discovered. The garden has been used for some time as the subject of an experiment in wine production, and has now been reopened to the public. The plaster casts have been restored in such a way as not to damage their natural appearance, and are on show in a new display case, lying on a bed of ashes and pumice.

Plaster casts of human bodies

THE BAKERY OF POPIDIUS PRISCUS AND THE LUPANAR

With the general improvements in the welfare of the population and the adoption of a life-style similar to that of the middle classes in larger cities, the baking of bread was no longer an activity confined to the home, as it originally had been.

Indeed, Pompeii boasted over thirty commercial bakeries (*pistrina*), easily recognizable by the presence of various millstones and a large oven. The millstone was made up of two pieces of hard, porous, grey lava. The lower part, known as the meta, was conical in form and fixed to the ground, while the upper section, the *catillus*, was hollow and shaped like an hourglass, with the top cone serving as a hopper. The grain was poured into the *catillus* and milled by means of rubbing together the two blocks; the flour was then collected in the trough underneath. There are two holes at the waist of the *catillus*: these were used to hold a wooden beam which was then attached to an animal. Following the milling process, the flour was dried and made into dough, which was rolled out on a board and shaped by hand. The final stage was the baking, and the larger bakeries had quite elaborate ovens of a considerable size. The bakery of Popidius Priscus communicated with his house; he came from one of the most illustrious families in Pompeii and the business was probably managed by one of his freedmen.

The lupanar, situated in the street of the same name, was the most important of the many brothels in Pompeii, and the only one which was expressly constructed for this function: the other houses of prostitution generally consisted of single rooms opening straight onto the street, or situated on the first floor of an inn. The lupanar extended over two floors, each with five rooms fitted with built-in masonry beds. Two of these rooms still carry erotic wall paintings. The prostitutes were slaves and the modest price paid for their services was pocketed by the procurer.

The Bakery of Popidius Priscus

THE HOUSE OF THE FAUN

The house takes its name from the elegant bronze statuette of a dancing faun which decorated one of its *impluviums* (the original, which has been substituted by a copy, can be seen in the Naples Archaeological Museum). The building covers an entire block and has a surface area of 3000 square metres, making it the largest house in Pompeii. For this reason, and because of its fine architecture and elegant decorations, it is classed as one of the most important examples of a private dwelling to have survived from antiquity. Unfortunately, only the barest vestiges of its former splendour still remain: the magnificent mosaics inspired by the feats of Alexander have been removed to the Naples Archaeological Museum, and the beautiful paintings in the first style have nearly all been lost.

The original layout of the house, dating back to the beginning of the 2nd century B.C. and built on the remains of a 3rd century house, already reflected the structure as we see it now. It shows a heavy Hellenistic influence and is based around two atriums (one of which was used to access the servants' quarters), a peristyle, and a garden: this was transformed into a second, larger, peristyle at the end of the 2nd century.

The main entrance had a tavern on either side and was fitted with a double door. The mosaic inscription of greeting in front of the doorway is in Latin (*Have*) instead of in Oscan, from which we can deduce that the owner supported the Romanization of the city. The vestibule has a coloured marble floor and contains two very fine

plasterwork lorariums. The atrium is in the Tuscan style and had a sophisticated *impluvium* in *opus sectile* inlay work, with coloured marble tiles cut to shape. At the back was the *tablinum*, decorated with a flooring of cubes which create an effect of perspective. On either side, are two dining-rooms, designed for use in the winter and decorated with mosaic pictures on the floor. The first peristyle features an elegant portico with 28 columns, and finishes in an exedra. At the entrance to this were some exotic mosaic pictures depicting creatures of the Nile, while inside was the extraordinary mosaic pavement showing the Battle of Alexander against Darius at Issus (now in the Naples Archaeological Museum). The image was copied from a very famous Hellenistic painting, perhaps by Philoxenos of Eretria, and was created in situ using about 1.5 million tiles, to cover an area of over 20 square metres. The main attention in the scene focuses on the naked panic of Darius, and his shocked, incredulous expression as he faces the unstoppable momentum of Alexander. The entire Persian army can be seen scattering around their king. The emotions of the characters are portrayed by means of some clever devices: Darius' desire for victory is further reinforced by the forward thrust of the spears (although these are seen to be thinning out behind him), while the Persian leader's charioteer is desperately whipping the fleeing horses as the Macedonian forces advance relentlessly. The exedra with the mosaic was flanked by two summer *tricliniums* and opened out onto a second vast peristyle with a garden. The servants' quarters were set conveniently apart, arranged around a tetrastyle atrium and equipped with a kitchen, bath and stable.

The vast peristyle in the House of the Faun

*Mosaic depicting the battle of Issus.
Detail: Alexander the Great*

THE HOUSE OF THE VETTII

This is one of the best preserved residences in Pompeii due to the fact that it was properly covered at the time of the first excavations in 1894. The owners were freedmen who ran a flourishing commercial concern. The original structure was built in the old style, as is shown by the monumental size of the front section, the cube-shaped capitals and the *impluvium* made of tuff. However, the building was remodelled in the 1st century A.D. and restored again after the earthquake. At the entrance is a painting of Priapus, the god of fertility, with his enormous phallus resting on a pair of scales, balanced by a bag full of money. The image was very much in the popular taste, protecting the house from the evil eye and bestowing prosperity on its owners. The huge

Aedicule with the image of the owner's Genius

atrium still bears some fine decoration in the fourth style, with cupids driving chariots, elaborate candelabra and children preparing sacrifices for the Penates, the protective spirits of the house. To the sides were discovered two strong wooden chests reinforced with iron and bronze. Among the various rooms opening off the atrium, the most striking are the *oecus* (main salon), decorated with mythological scenes, and a *cubiculum*, which has paintings of various types of edible fish. The living area was arranged around the peristyle, which became the centre of the house after the *tablinum* (reception room) was removed. The most important rooms looked onto a very elaborate garden, with jets of water gushing from fanciful statues and feeding into basins.

Triclinium: on the left, painting with Pentheus torn apart by the Maenads; *on the right* The Punishment of Dirce

This was in line with the current fashion during the imperial age, by which the owners of city mansions copied the design of plants and sculptures typical of luxury suburban villas. The *oecus* contains some excellent paintings in the fourth style. These mythological scenes, together with the murals in the other rooms, constitute a real picture gallery, made up of copies of famous Greek originals. The *triclinium* is famous for its spectacular decoration in the fourth style: set against a brilliant "Pompeii red" background are some classic images taken from Greek masterpieces.

These are inserted in panels and framed by imaginary architecture, and depict *Daedalus and Pasiphae*, *Ixion tied to the wheel*, and *Dionysus and Ariadne*. However, it is in the composition of the friezes and ornamental motifs that the painters have left us the best proof of their creativity, with figures and perspectives rendered with an expert lightness of touch. The most striking room in this respect is the *oecus*, where the frieze on a black field sets off the huge vermilion backdrops on the walls. The vertical panels depict elements of imaginary architecture, while the horizontal sections show a series of mythological figures, cupids and *psychai* (winged deities) engaged in games or different crafts (goldsmiths, fullers, perfumers, etc.). The Hellenistic concept is tempered by a more casual and rustic element in the Roman mode, achieving an unusual degree of balance and tension between the styles.

The rooms to the right of the *triclinium*, framed by an elegant little portico, may have been used as a *gynaecium* (women's section). The servants' quarters were arranged on two floors around a second atrium, dominated by a large *lararium* in the form of an aedicule. In the neighbouring kitchen, some bronze pans were discovered still standing on top of the stove next to the sink. The small room next door, whose purpose is still unknown, is decorated with pictures of erotic themes which are painted in a very simple style. A statue of Priapus, which once had water spouting from his phallus, completed the interior decoration.

Garden and peristyle of the House of the Vettii

THE HOUSE OF THE DIOSCURI

The house was the result of combining previous dwellings fronting onto Via di Mercurio, probably during the imperial era. The original structures, still recognizable, were incorporated to create an original and evocative design. The interior decorations, with paintings in the fourth style, make it one of the most prestigious patrician residences in Pompeii. The entrance opens onto a magnificent Corinthian atrium, embellished with a portico with twelve tuff columns coated in plaster. The surrounding rooms were decorated by the same workshop involved in the House of the Vettii. There are some spectacular motifs and decorative patterns, with copies of famous pictures of mythological themes and human figures depicted on a large scale (the most important of these, such as Pan and Hermaphroditus, are now in the Naples Archaeological Museum). These decorations indicate the care taken by the wealthy purchaser

to surround himself with a setting sufficiently magnificent to impress his guests. The *tablinum* faces onto a portico with Doric columns which contained the *sacellum* (shrine) for the *lararium*. A second peristyle opens out to the right of the atrium, containing two basins with fountains and adorned with decorations in the fourth style, still visible on the walls. The east side is left open to ensure the *oecus* remains visible. This room, used as a sitting-room and reception area, is decorated with elements of fake architecture set against a white ground and paintings of still life. The large paintings on the pillars at the entrance (*Medea contemplating the murder of her children; Perseus and Andromeda*) are now in the Naples Archaeological Museum. From the peristyle, one can access the servant's quarters, created by the incorporation of another house with Tuscan atrium, quite independent from the main residence.

Painting showing Perseus and Andromeda

Peristyle of the House of the Dioscuri

HOUSE OF THE SMALL FOUNTAIN AND OF THE LARGE FOUNTAIN

This is one of the most important houses dating from the Samnite era. The traditional entrance made from square blocks of tuff led into a large, imposing atrium with a dark floor decorated with small white chips. The various rooms led off this. The atrium was designed for entertaining *clientes*, and had to be grand to reflect the social position of the owner. He would have received them standing on the threshold of the *tablinum*, silhouetted against the garden behind. This part of the building, remodelled in the post-Augustan period with the enlargement of the garden, constituted the central focus of the house. Due to the limited space available, only a partial colonnade could be built, leaving it to the painter to use his powers of illusion to make the area seem larger. The wall at the back is adorned with a charming fountain-nymphaeum in the form of a little temple, which

has a grotto-style apse flanked by two statues (copies). It is decorated with glass-paste mosaics in shades of blue and green with red and white details, and these include the famous siren. A painting stretches along the walls on either side of the nymphaeum, seeming to prolong the colonnade by the use of ingenious perspective. Thanks to a very clever and precise pictorial technique, the view appears to extend over imaginary maritime landscapes, with improbable bridges, ports and vessels.

The adjoining House of the Large Fountain is very similar, with the fountain-nymphaeum constituting the main focus of the surrounding garden. This type of design was borrowed from the large suburban villas, and an attempt was made to copy their original size and splendour, using pictorial devices to "extend" the limitations of the pokier city houses.

Fountain-nymphaeum in the House of the small Fountain

The peristyle of the House of the small Fountain with illusionistic paintings

THE HOUSE OF THE TRAGIC POET AND THE HOUSE OF MELEAGER

Although only of a modest size, the House of the Tragic Poet is a typical example of the sort of home owned by the increasingly affluent middle class in the last years of life of the city. The two taverns standing on either side of the entrance indicate that the owner was probably involved in business. The most characteristic feature of the house is the mosaic in front of the doorway depicting a dog on a chain and bearing the message *Cave canem* (beware of the dog). The *cubicula* were arranged around the atrium, from where you could access the upper floor. In both the atrium and the peristyle were some important artworks with heroic and mythical themes, including the dramatic painting of the *Sacrifice of Iphigenia*. The mosaic from which the house takes its name, showing a *choragus* (narrator) instructing a group of actors, was originally in the *tablinum*, and is now in the Naples Archaeological Museum. The *tablinum* gave onto a modest garden, surrounded by a small portico, at the end of which was a *lararium* in the form of a small temple. On the right was a simple kitchen next to a large *triclinium* decorated with paintings: *Venus looking at a nest of cherubs, Ariadne abandoned* and *Stories of Diana*.

Other pictures can be found in the rooms on the opposite side: *Ariadne and Theseus, Venus fishing* and *Narcissus at the spring*.

The House of Meleager is composed of the combination of two previous homes centred on a Tuscan atrium and a peristyle. The *oecus*, which was lent extra dignity by the addition of a colonnade, was adorned with lively decorations in the fourth style including imaginary architectural elements, masks, satyrs and female figures, between which several paintings were hung. In the impressive *triclinium*, which has a very unusual architectural and pictorial design, plaster is used to give added volume to the painted areas.

Mosaic in front of the doorway of the House of the Tragic Poet with the writing Cave canem

THE HOUSE OF APOLLO

The House of Apollo owes its name to the many representations of this god which have been found inside. The façade has the limestone appearance of houses of the Samnite era, while the interior reflects the demands of the patrician class in the final phase of Pompeii. The layout of the house is irregular, due to the various additions made in the first century A.D., which involved enlarging the atrium and adding a garden. The Tuscan atrium opens onto a *tablinum*, and it was here that the statuettes of Apollo and of the Faun with a deer were discovered (the originals are in the Naples Archaeological Museum). This room was decorated with extremely elegant pictures in the fourth style, showing Venus with her mirror, and the injured Adonis, set at the centre of panels framed by delicate architectural motifs.

The two rooms on the left, which can be accessed by some steps, were included at the expense of the neighbouring house. In the small courtyard stood an elegant pyramid-shaped fountain, over-laid in marble and decorated with little statues. This opened onto a large *triclinium* with a pavement in *opus sectile*. The adjacent garden with a summer *triclinium*, positioned at a lower level, once made up part of the neighbouring dwelling: a green area planted with flowers and shrubs surrounded a raised bath with a fountain.

On the walls of the garden were three important glass-paste mosaics bordered by shells: *Achilles being recognised by Ulysses on Skyros* remains in situ, while the *Three Graces* and *Achilles confronting Agamemnon* are now in the Naples Archaeological Museum. The *triclinium* was sheltered by a columned portico and had a mosaic floor and wall decorations showing birds and plants on a red background, now in a poor state of repair. The nearby *cubiculum* with two alcoves, decorated with scenes from the myth of Apollo, was probably used for leisure pursuits. It featured the sort of ornate multi-coloured decoration which typified the extravagant tastes of the time of Nero.

Frescoes in fourth style in the House of Apollo

VILLA OF DIOMEDES

This imposing residence takes its name, quite inappropriately, from the nearby tomb of M. Arrius Diomedes. The villa was built in the 2nd century B.C. and subsequently remodelled after the founding of the colony. The front of the building is at an acute angle in relation to the street: a quirk which provides a good demonstration of the way the old aristocracy generally reorganized their properties after the arrival of the Roman settlers. An entrance with a small *prothyrum* (porch portal) opened onto a large peristyle. To the left of this, there was a small portico leading to a bath area, with an adjacent kitchen and various rooms for residential or service use. On the south side was an impressive *cubiculum* with an apse and three large windows, preceded by an anteroom. It contained a small bedroom and was probably used by the owner. Situated on the west side was a *tablinum*, through which one could access a large *triclinium*,
built on an underlying structure. This room was open to the sea, in line with the Hellenistic taste for communing with the surrounding landscape.

A flight of steps led to the lower section of the villa, scenically positioned on a slope descending to the sea and supported by a cryptoportico, used as a cellar. The bodies of various victims were discovered here, including the daughter and wife of the owner, together with their servants. They were carrying money and jewellery with them as they attempted to flee the eruption. This part of the villa included a large garden, surrounded on four sides by a peristyle, at the centre of which was a basin with fountain and a summer *triclinium*.

The arrangement of the villa on several levels and the unusual layout of the rooms, probably determined by the wishes of the wealthy owner, make this residence one of the most interesting experiments in architecture to be found in Pompeii.

VILLA OF THE MYSTERIES

The villa takes its name from the paintings to be found in the *triclinium*, and has been progressively restored form 1929 onwards. It belonged to the wealthy Istacidi family, whose impressive tomb can be seen near Herculaneum Gate. With its unusual architectural design and its exceptional cycle of paintings, it ranks as one of the most important building to have survived in Pompeii. The original building dates from the 2nd century B.C., but was redesigned in the following century. A farmhouse section was added in the 1st century A.D. The property therefore consists of a very large, square structure divided into a farm section, which produced wine, and luxury residential quarters overlooking the sea. The entrance takes one into a large peristyle with the various sections leading off it. The living quarters were arranged around a series of rooms made up of an atrium, *tablinum* and salon and ending in a circular exedra with large windows which faces onto the sea. This part was encircled by a hanging garden built on a wide terrace. Because of the steep incline, this was raised on an artificial embankment surrounded by a large cryptoportico. The decoration in the 2nd style, dating from a refurbishment carried out in about 60 B.C., has been excellently preserved. It creates a very effective illusion, using elements of real architecture. The *tablinum* was decorated with fine pictures in the 3rd style painted on a black ground; the two-dimensional figures show a strong Egyptian influence. The *cubicula* contain decorations in the second style showing scenes from the Dionysiac cycle (see page 92): the malicious figure of the dancing satyr is particularly vivid. A bath complex could be entered from the peristyle and was located next to kitchen courtyard. The farming section of the building included many rooms for servants and a *torcularium* containing two wine-presses.

External view of the Villa of the Mysteries

Villa of the Mysteries: the atrium

THE DIONYSIAC CYCLE OF PAINTINGS

This impressive *megalographia* (painting on a grand theme) covers all the walls of a room in the Villa of the Mysteries. The work is based on a Hellenistic model and is one of the most famous surviving examples of ancient art. There is some uncertainty as to the subject matter, but it could concern rites of initiation for women into marriage or the Dionysiac mysteries. The figures are arranged along a high podium and set against a brilliant red background, separated by a series of vertical strips sustaining a cornice. It is thought that the sequence should be read from left to right. This seems to be implied by the stance of the imposing female figure, advancing towards the couple with the seated girl and the child reading – often thought to represent the young Dionysus. The female figure alongside has her head turned towards the viewer and is carrying a tray which may bear sacred offerings. Next come three women grouped around at a table: the one with her back to us, probably a priestess, is performing certain rites invisible to the observer. There follows an aged Silenus crowned with laurels and playing the lyre, who is accompanied by two satyrs: the male is playing the pan pipes and the female is offering her breast to a deer. A figure wearing a cloak blowing in the wind introduces the next group: an aged Silenus is holding a cup, into which is peering a young satyr, and his companion is raising a theatrical mask. The next sequence shows a drunken Dionysus, leaning feebly on the breast of Ariadne. A young man is caught in the act of exposing his phallus (symbolic of the fertile power of nature), while a majestic winged demon in the shape of a woman is seen whipping a girl, who seeks refuge on the lap of another woman. To the right, a naked maiden is dancing and playing the cymbals. In the following scene, peace is restored: a girl is preparing for her wedding, combing her hair with assistance from her maid. The lone figure with staring eyes, who brings the cycle to a close, could well be the lady of the house.

The Dionysiac cycle of paintings

INDEX OF NAMES

PHOTOGRAPHS

Giovanni Lattanzi / Archart 19, 21, 29, 31, 35, 51, 53, 54, 57, 59, 61, 77, 80, 85, 91

Mimmo Jodice/CORBIS 87

Luca Mozzati 6, 7, 8, 9, 10, 13, 22, 24, 25, 26, 32, 33, 34, 36, 37, 39, 40, 41, 42, 46, 47, 48, 49, 55, 60, 62, 63, 65, 71, 73, 74, 76, 82, 83, 84, 90,

Picture Library DeAgostini 11, 14, 15, 23, 27, 45, 64, 75, 79, 93

The Photographer-Thomas Camp 81

Erika Zucchetti 69

Illustrazioni di Giorgio Albertini 16, 17, 21, 25, 27, 29, 31, 33, 43, 45, 49, 51, 55, 59, 66, 67, 79, 91

Organization and production
Ellisse s.a.s. di Sergio Abate & C. - via Soffredini 65, Milano

Thanks to Tiziana Rocco for the scientific review

This volume was printed for Mondadori Electa S.p.A.
at Elcograf S.p.A., via Mondadori 15, Verona, in the year 2013